PENGUIN BOOKS

TO GRILL A MOCKINGBIRD

Mitchell Rose lives in San Francisco and spends too much time thinking about food.

Ruth Young also lives in San Francisco and divides her time between her food processor and her word processor.

TO GRILL A MOCKINGBIRD

AND OTHER TASTY TITLES

Concocted and Illustrated by
Ruth Young and Mitchell Rose

PENGUIN BOOKS

PENGUIN BOOKS
Viking Penguin Inc., 40 West 23rd Street,
New York, New York 10010, U.S.A.
Penguin Books Ltd, Harmondsworth,
Middlesex, England
Penguin Books Australia Ltd, Ringwood,
Victoria, Australia
Penguin Books Canada Limited, 2801 John Street,
Markham, Ontario, Canada L3R 1B4
Penguin Books (N.Z.) Ltd, 182–190 Wairau Road,
Auckland 10, New Zealand

First published in Penguin Books 1985

Published simultaneously in Canada

LIBRARY OF CONGRESS CATALOGING IN PUBLICATION DATA
Young, Ruth.
To grill a mockingbird and other tasty titles.
1. Titles of books—Anecdotes, facetiae, satire, etc.
2. Puns and punning. I. Rose, Mitchell. II. Title.
PN6231.T65Y68   1985   818'.5407   84-18931
ISBN 0 14 00.7744 8

Printed in the United States of America by
R. R. Donnelley & Sons Company, Harrisonburg, Virginia
Set in Aster

To my father, who taught me how
to laugh,
and my mother, who taught me
how to eat
                    —R.Y.

For Arlette and Gus
                    —M.R.

TO GRILL A MOCKINGBIRD

TO GRILL A MOCKINGBIRD

The complete book of Small Bird Cookery and Poultry Appetizers, by Mini Sheraton. Includes recipes for Crepes Canary, Filet of Finch, Stuffed Sparrow, and Parakeet Patties.

"A small classic"   —*The Avian Review*

GORKY PORK

by Martin Smithfield-Hamm

In 1943, German armies retreating from Russia took with them many treasures, among them a secret Czarist recipe for "Gorky Pork." Forty years later, an American journalist in Baden-Baden accidentally stumbles upon the recipe and is found murdered. Why is it so important that two great powers are driven to the brink of nuclear war to possess it? On the case are Natasha Piroshki, Head Dietitian for the KGB, and Stan Kasha, CIA agent. Their inevitable confrontation in a Paris *charcuterie* provides the searing climax to this international tidbit of intrigue and heartburn.

"When it comes to pork, no one writes better than Smithfield-Hamm."   —Francis Bacon

"Even better than *The Spy Who Came In for the Coldcuts*"

Dip
of
Fools

The new novel by the winner of the 1982 Nobowl Prize for Fingerfoods—an allegorical account of a cocktail party that serves up an appetizing array of characters: from the blandest cheese to the hottest guacamole, the types are all here—those mixed gently, not so gently, and the ones that were clearly chilled eight hours before serving.

The Scarlet Pumpernickel

Intrigue and high adventure in a Paris *boulangerie* during the French Revolution—the story of a daring hero disguised as an unassuming, unbleached, unbolted rye bread.

"Fresh!"

"Great with a little butter"

—*The Whole Wheat Catalog*

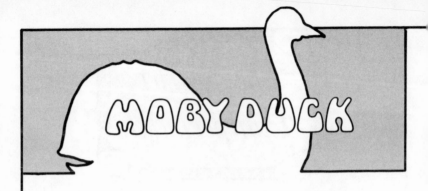

MOBY DUCK

"Call me Fishmeal," begins this monumental novel, which is both a tale of wild-game-bird hunting and a symbolic study of good and bad manners. Moby Duck is pursued by the monomaniacal Captain Ahem, world-class arbiter of table etiquette. Ahem's greasy fingers bear witness to his last encounter with the great white duck.

———————

"Rubbed with salt and pepper and garnished with thin slices of orange, this book is in the best of taste!"

THE MALTESE FLANKEN

Dashiell Omelette's latest hard-boiled thriller. When his partner is found dead of indigestion with a half-eaten brisket of beef sandwich clutched in his hand, Sam Spread goes off in search of the killer and a decent pickle.

"Omelette's best since *The Glass Quiche*"
—*Deli World*

Drumsticks
Along the Mohawk

The story of the first fast-food franchise in America,
two hundred years before The Colonel.

"A bucketful of little-known history"

—Studs Turkey

Alice's Adventure in Wonder Bread

A delightful reminiscence that takes us back to those pre-wholegrain days when the little grocer on the corner still had his shelves stacked with Devil Dogs, Hydrox cookies, and, of course, packaged white bread.

"Made me want to run into the kitchen and make a ketchup sandwich."

Grimm's Fairy Snails

A new edition of an old children's classic, including "Goldy Lox and the Three Beers," "Monterey Jack and the Beansprout," "The Goose That Laid the Hard-Boiled Egg," and "Hansel and Pretzel."

THE CARROTS
OF
WIMPOLE STREET

A complex family melodrama involving four generations of carrots and some neighboring squash. Later
turned into the hit TV miniseries *Roots*.

"Will enhance your vision."

One Flew Over the Chicken's Breast

***The* Institutional Cookbook.**

"The section on cooking brains is worth the price alone."

"I'm nuts about this book."   —Ken Queasy

A CLAM FOR ALL SEASONS

A heartwarming story of the struggle of one man against nature. This is the authorized biography of Barney Kull, the man responsible for breeding the bivalves that resulted in a clam that can be eaten even in months that don't have *r*'s. SOON TO BE A MAJOR CHOWDER.

CRY, THE BELOVED POULTRY

First in a projected three-part autobiography of famous Bird Colonels.

"Finger-lickin' readin' "

—*Chicken Science Monitor*

TRAVELS WITH BARLEY

The prize-winning vegetarian author of *Grapes of Broth* delights us once more with this account of his trip across America. A galloping romp that mushrooms into real adventure! Cerealized in this month's *New York Review of Cooks*.

"Soup is good reading."

The Marzipan Chronicles

BY RAY WHEATBERRY

Two space travelers from Earth, wandering across the bleak landscape of Mars, discover the ruins of a long-dead civilization—a civilization that brought the art of confectionery making to a height never achieved on Earth—and then decay set in . . . *why*?

"Wheatberry's bittersweet tale is a lesson for all of us."   —*American Dental Association Journal*

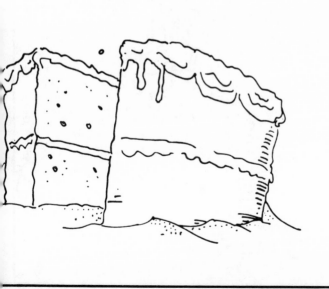

Lady Chatterley's Liver

Called "tasteless" by the censors of her day, here is Constance Chatterley's searing story, rich in hunting and fishing lore and vitamin B! It's all here—her husband, her gamekeeper, her iron-deficiency anemia—dredged in frank language and smothered in onions!

Chow Mein Street

The author penetrates beneath the surface of a middle-priced Chinese restaurant to reveal a world filled with heartburn and MSG.

"Half an hour after finishing this book, I wanted to read another one."

THE POULTRY OF ALLEN GINSBIRD

Collected works, including the classic "Fowl."

Finnegans Steak

The author of *Portrait of the Artist as a Young Ham* has written another dazzlingly complex novel set in a Dublin butcher shop. Using puns, slang, song titles, syllables from every imaginable linguistic source, plus prime beef, James Juice treats us to extravagant language you can really sink your teeth into.

"Rare!"

"Well done!"

"Grade-A writing!"

FEAR OF FRYING

Enter the audacious, uninhibited, foxy, frisky world of psychiatrist's wife Isadora Chickenwing, and follow her from the frying pan to the fire.

———

"Polly Unsaturate at her sizzling best!"

"If you want to meet strangers on trains, this is the best manual I know."

𝕿𝖍𝖊 𝕭𝖚𝖓𝖘 𝖔𝖋 𝕬𝖚𝖌𝖚𝖘𝖙

A sweeping historical drama based on the attempt by the German bread industry to change the eating habits of Europe with the introduction of the Kaiser roll.

THE
INTERPRETATION
OF
GREENS

A massive volume that finally answers the question: "Do vegetables talk?" Translated from the original Spinach.

THE
SCARLET
LETTUCE

Long banned, this book gives us a compassionate and compelling account of the world of seventeenth-century Boston greengrocers. You'll not soon forget Hester Prynne, condemned to wear both Bibb and Red Leaf lettuce around her neck by Roger Chillingworth (a real iceberg), as punishment for not finishing her salad.

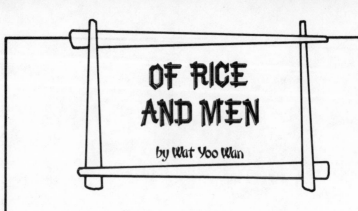

OF RICE AND MEN

by Wat Yoo Wan

The story of Chinese takeout food in America, this book is a combination of drama, humor, and egg roll.

"Well worth waiting for"

LORD
of the
ONION
RINGS

A deep-fried guide to Who's Who in Middle Earth, full of names, facts, dates, maps, special languages, genealogical tables for two, four, or larger parties with advance notice.

EL SQUID

Eight gripping tales, all set on the island of Calamari.

"Tough"

"Not for the squeamish"

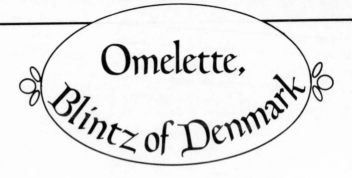

Omelette, Blintz of Denmark

A melancholy Danish prince becomes a royal pain to his mother and uncle, egging the guilty pair on while pretending to be cracked. Young Omelette's great soliloquy, closing with the words:

> The pie's the thing! Now watch!
> I'll throw the custard at the King!

brings the curtain down on the messiest pie-throwing melee in theater history.

ALL THE PRESIDENT'S HENS

A detailed account of the pecking order of Richard M. Nixon's White House.

HEDDA COBBLER

The best-selling author of *An Enemy of the Pickle, A Dill's House,* and *Peer Gherkin* departs from his now familiar themes to concoct a steaming story of Scandinavian scandal. Meet Hedda—a deep dish—and Lövbored, the peach farmer who loved but bored her.

Brittle Women

A powerful, unforgettable tale of four sisters growing up on a Georgia peanut farm, and the tragic results. . . .

"It will break your heart into pieces."

The Derma Bums

The story of Ginsbird's Deli, the birthplace of The Beet Generation. An American odyssey of poets, visionaries, and noshers seeking the ultimate high and the perfect knish. They're all here . . . Jack Caraway . . . Gregory Kasha . . . and, of course, Ginsbird himself.

"A classic to be placed alongside *Remembrance of Things Pastrami*"   —*Kishka Review*

Leo Tolstoy's myth-shattering novel about aggression and legumes. Set during the Napoleonic invasion of Russia, this book proves that the pan is mightier than the sword. Over five hundred characters crowd the pages (they didn't call him Count Tolstoy for nothing!).

———

"Tamara Leftova is unforgettable—a fully rounded character."

THE SOUFFLÉ ALSO RISES

Set in the decadent court of Louis XIV, this is the story of a lowly soufflé who rises to become the King's favorite dish.

"Whisks you away!"

The Adventures of HAMHOCK BONES

The mysteries of soul cooking revealed!

A SEPARATE PIZZA

Insights into America's fastest-growing food craze. Chapters include:

- —Here or to Go?
- —What to Do When You Love Anchovies and Your Partner Doesn't
- —New York or Chicago: Which Is Best?
- —How to Order Extras
- —101 Combinations

HEARTBURN of DARKNESS

"The horror, the horror . . ."

"Searing!"

"The Belchin' Congo as never seen before"

Condensed in *Reader's Digestion*.

THE PICKWICK PEPPERS

Dickens fans won't want to miss this pack of piquant peppers, stuffed, stewed, and marinated in humbug. If you liked *Halvah Twist*, you'll love *Pickwick Peppers*!

First time in pepperback!

Fillet It As It Lays

A history of boning, from the ancient mammoth boners of eastern Siberia to the amazing sardine skinners and boners of today's Portugal.

———

"The only bone I have to pick with this book is that it wasn't long enough."

More aggressive than anything that's come down the pike in years, this is an incredibly raw, tough book that offers a firsthand account of life in the freezer.

"Fathom thousands packed in like sardines
—the author's rage is no fluke."

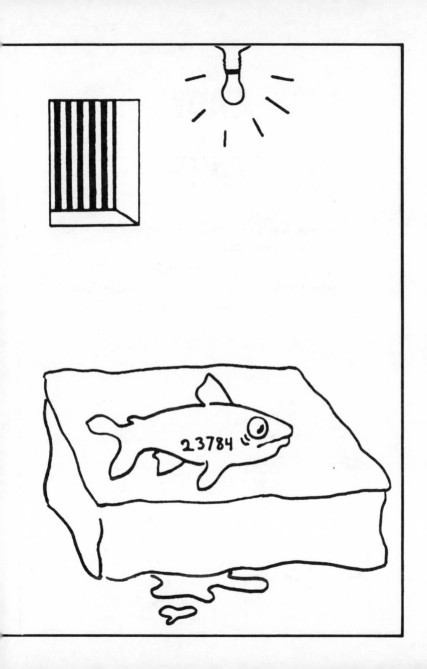

The
LADY
in the
CAKE

A stark look into the world of stag parties and American Legion get-togethers.

"A real surprise!" —Betty Cracker

CRIME AND NOURISHMENT

A novel sociological study of criminals and their diets. The chapter on "Fingerfoods and Pickpockets" is particularly insightful.

———

"I couldn't put this book down."
—former shoplifter, name withheld

cheeses of NAZARETH

The story of Biblical cheeses by the author of *The Dead Sea Rolls*.

"Inspiring"

THE FRENCH-FRIED CONNECTION

Set along the interstates and off-ramps of the Southwest, this gut-rending drama of a junk-food addict's descent into the greasy world of fast food is recommended only to readers with strong stomachs.

"Crackles like the fat on a greasy spoon's grill."
—ABC's *Oily Morning News*

Sex and Tempurament

No need to give up on either!

Margaret Mood's indispensable study provides an easy way to discuss the previously undiscussable. Early chapters cover diverse topics such as:

—Cranky Hanky Panky
—Why men and women often miss the best deep-fried vegetables of their lives

———————

"Reading this book is the next best thing."

East of Edam

A tour de force about a big wheel surrounded by semi-soft sycophants and the cracker who loves him.

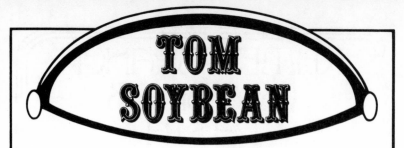

TOM SOYBEAN

The runaway bestseller about making it big in the commodities market.

———

"No whitewashing here"

REMEMBRANCE OF THINGS PASTA

The full account by Fettucini himself of his life and art—from his debut at an unknown pizza parlor on the outskirts of Naples to the restless, brilliant years in Milan when he brought noodles to the world. A lifelong love story, includes never-before-published interviews with Gnocchi, Alfredo, Vermicelli, others.

"Al dente con tutto!"

Spuds
Lonigan

A cautionary tale about crime and carbohydrates.

I Remember Marmalade

An emotionally stirring recollection of the American Army Preserves during the Second World War.

THE BLACK SCALLION

Generations of children have loved this tale of a ship-wrecked young boy whose life is saved by a giant, very dark green onion, on which he floats to safety. On their lush, uninhabited island, boy and onion live peacefully until they are rescued and returned to civilization.

"Uninhibited and often raw account of friendship, survival, and the never-to-be-underestimated importance of mouthwash"

The World According to Carp

Smash nationwide bestseller by a writer's writer! Meet T. S. (Terribly Salable) Carp, porpoiseful young novelist, and discover the best love story New England has produced since *Ethan Fromage*.

voyage of the bagel

At last! Charles Darwin as he really was—the long-awaited firsthand account by that world-class naturalist and nosher of his historic Australian voyage. Inspired by the crew's keeping kosher, Darwin saw the link between bagels and cream cheese, which he later described as Survival of the Fattest. Includes his Theory of Natural Selection: Plain or Onion, Sesame, Poppy, Whole Wheat, Pumpernickel, Egg, or Raisin.

"A worthy follow-up to *The Origin of Spices*!"

PITA PAN

A fairytale about a young Middle Eastern hero, Pita, who has run away to Never-Leaven-Land to escape rising up to full maturity. Here he lives in the trees with the fairies and some hummus, and travels around on Flying Saucer bread.

"Stuffed with adventure and fresh garbanzo beans!"

BEANS AND NOTHINGNESS

The first major statement by a French existentialist on the nature of social flatulence since *Wind, Sand and Stars*, this examination of the hows and whys of legumes is Jean-Paul Sartre's attempt to systematize his thinking on man's condition regarding self-consciousness and gas. "Face it," Sartre tells us, "existence precedes flatulence."

Karl Marx's principles of Dietetic Materialism applied to all aspects of café life. Percolating for years, Marx filtered and ground down earlier theories *(Das Coffee-cake)* into this stirring work, which had great influence on the development of coffee klatches everywhere. It represents his thinking from 1860 to 1864, after which he stopped thinking and organized the first Tupperware Party.

———

"Strong—no sugar"

WEBSTER'S STANDARD UNABRIDGED Confectionery

HERE IT IS!—everything you've always wanted to know about sucrose, lactose, glucose, and fructose.

———————

"I spent the better part of a night drooling over this book."

THE NAKED AND THE BREAD

Recipes from the nudist colonies of southern California. The author, who has spent fifteen years collecting these mouth-watering recipes, now reveals all.

"Buns of fun"   —*Rolling Scone*

GRAND
HOTILLAMOOK

Long-awaited, this book gives us a shocking look into the famed Hollywood fat farm for gratinée idols and semisoft starlets.

The
Whitefish
Hotel

The soleful story of Anna S., a young woman whose suffering from migraine haddocks has made her hard of herring. This is the moving account of her treatment by a famous Viennese sturgeon.

"Hard to remember, but impossible to forget"

"As edible as it is Oedipal"

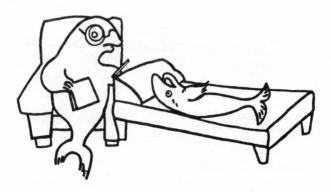

Little Couscous on the Prairie

The first of the "Little Couscous" books that children have been eating for decades.

———————

"Laura Semolina Wilder at her most delicious!"

100 YEARS OF SOLID FOOD

The authorized biography of José Buendiet, South American food theorist. What you can do *NOW* to achieve Optimal Life Duration (O.L.D.).

"The diet for longevity we've all been waiting for"

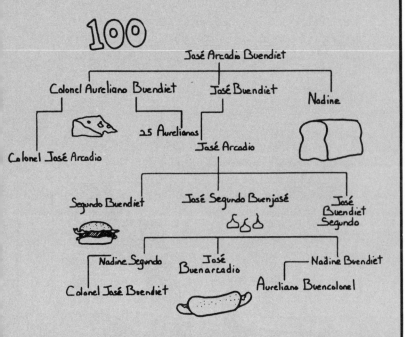

THE BIG LEEK

The plush, celebrity-filled restaurants of Beverly Hills are a far cry from the hamburger joints of downtown L.A. But when Jean-Paul Vichyssoise is found murdered by an eight-foot leek that kills with bad breath, Philip Marshmallow jumps in his beat-up old Mustang and heads for Rodeo Drive.

"Once again, Raymond Colander brings us cold-blooded murder served up piping hot."

WHAT COLOR IS YOUR PARMESAN?

A comprehensive, up-to-date guide for cheese hunters. "If you're fed up with Feta, tired of Tilsit, and bored with Brie, this is the book for you."

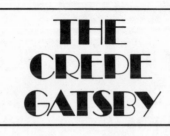

THE CREPE GATSBY

An American love story set against the background of suburban Long Island. Meet industrialist Jay Gatsby, the Breakfast-Cookware King; his neighbor, Nick Caraway (for whom he named Crepes Nicholas); and finally, Daisy, who drove him, flaming with Cointreau, rum, or cognac, to distraction.

"Passion and ambition at the dawn of the Teflon industry"

"Exposes French Pancakes for their false glamour, nutritional emptiness, and inflated price."

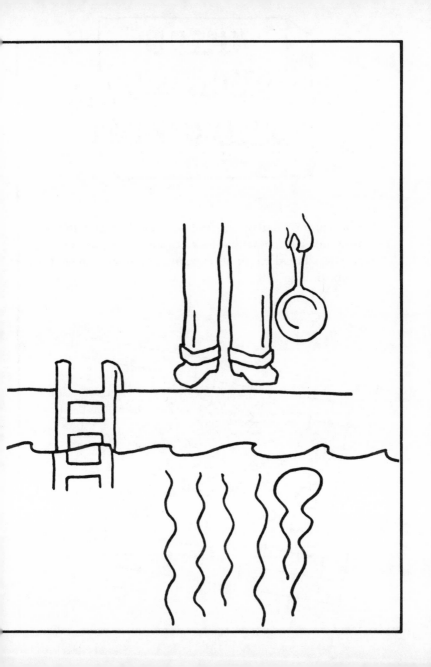

THE ADMIRABLE CROUTON

Set in a tiny salad on the south coast of England, this story takes a compelling look at those little pieces of crustless bread we've all encountered at some point in our dining.

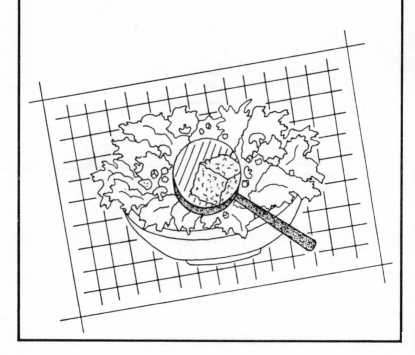

The Little Quince

Juicy pulp novel about a small fruit who gets into a big jam.

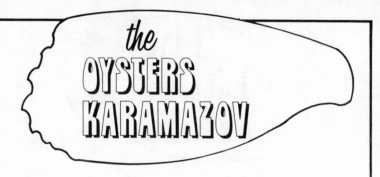

the OYSTERS KARAMAZOV

The story of a shellfish, dissolute father and his bivalve sons, set in the shallow waters of nineteenth-century Russia.

"Highly edible *and* low in calories!"

"A pearl!"

An Ale
of Two Cities

Lucy Manette, daughter of Dr. Alexander Manette of Milwaukee and St. Louis, hops from danger to disaster in Charles Dickens's masterful tale of beer and revolution, is finally rescued by Sydney Carton, the man responsible for first liberating mankind from the weighty keg, and later, for light beer. "It is a far, far lighter lager that I drink than I have ever drunk before" is Carton's unforgettable last line.

"Great taste —less filling"

Which of these books have you been meaning to eat?

The Oxtail Incident
On the Watercress
Halvah Twist
Androcles and the Loinchop
A Majority of Won Ton
Breakfast of Champignons
Mary Popcorn
The Catsup in the Rye
Pride and Prune Juice
Far from the Pudding Crowd
From Beer to Infirmity
Day of the Loquat
A Farewell to Artichokes

Splendor in the Foie Gras
The Continental Pop
Tabasco Road
For Whom the Jelly Rolls
The Tart Is a Lonely Hunter
Salad of the Bad Café*
The World of Sushi Wong
The Taming of the Stew
Porkloin's Complaint
Judgment at Nuremburger
Confessions of Felix Cruller
Huckleberry Gin
Anne of Green Bagles*
Uncle Tom's Cabbage*

*Warning: May Cause Heartburn

Take any four only $1 each

with membership in the Culinary Guild